THE 3x3
INTERVIEW PREP METHOD

How to Land Your Dream Job on Wall $treet

BRIAN ROGERS

Edited by Bill Gaythwaite

Illustrations, front and back cover designs by Brian Rogers

theROGERSgroup nyc

www.rogersgroupnyc.net

theROGERSgroup nyc

Copyright ©2017 by Brian Rogers. All rights reserved. New York, New York

Printed in the United States of America. Except as permitted under the United States Copyright Act of 1976, no part of this publication may be reproduced in any form or by any means, or stored in a database or retrieval system, without prior written permission of the author.

This publication is designed to provide accurate and authoritative information in regard to the subject matter covered. It is sold with the understanding that the publisher is not engaged in rendering legal, accounting, or other professional service. If legal advice or other expert assistance is required, the services of a competent professional should be sought.

—From a Declaration of Principles jointly adopted by a committee of the American Bar Association and a committee of publishers and associations

ISBN: 978-1-5446-3000-7

To my loves, my little monkeys
Joaquin and Olivia

Acknowledgments

My dad Robert has been pushing me to write this book for years now so in many ways this is as much his baby as it is mine. Thanks for pressing on Grandpa Bobby.

Thanks to my mom Beverly who has been my biggest source of inspiration and motivation. She's always been my most loyal fan, greatest supporter and I'm blessed to have her in my life. You are an amazing woman and a role model for us all.

Thanks to my brother Billy for still talking to me after all the big brother abuse he took from me growing up together. I've never met anyone with more friends or the ability to make friends faster and live a fun life than Billy and it's taught me a lot.

A special thanks to Professor Irving Schenkler who for years has run the Management Communication Department at NYU Stern. I was Irv's business communication student and teaching assistant while getting my MBA then later Irv gave me the chance to teach my first business communication class in 2012, it changed my life forever.

A toast to the iron ladies: my great grandmother Bernice M. Rogers, my mom Beverly Colvin, my great-aunt Beverly Brady and my junior high English teacher Mrs. Anna Southard. I am who I am because of these bad-ass women.

Bill Gaythwaite did an amazing job helping me with the editing and I will always be grateful for his work.

Any and all mistakes, typos, errors or general stupidity in this book are mine and mine alone.

Contents

Preface i
Introduction xv

Part 1 - Overview of the 3x3 Method 1
Chapter 1 - The Company 5
Chapter 2 - The Job 9
Chapter 3 - The Candidate 11
Chapter 4 - Understanding the Candidate: Story Development for Each Bullet 15
Chapter 5 - Develop an Elevator Pitch 24

Part 2 - Maximizing Your Presence 27
Chapter 6 - How to Walk into the Room with Confidence 35
Chapter 7 - Four Parts of the Voice 40
Chapter 8 - Seated Posture, Eye Contact & Facial Expressions 48
Chapter 9 - Hand Gestures 52

Part 3 - Handshakes, Questions, Pressure and Practice 55
Chapter 10 - Handshakes 57
Chapter 11 - What Questions Should You Ask Them? 62
Chapter 12 - The Closer's Question 64
Chapter 13 - Mock Interviewing and Using Video to Practice 69
Chapter 14 - Stay Cool Under Pressure: 6 Tips to Help You Stay Calm 74

Afterword 83
Index 85
About the Author 87

Preface

Nothing in this world can take the place of persistence.
Talent will not; nothing is more common than unsuccessful men with talent.
Genius will not; unrewarded genius is almost a proverb.
Education will not; the world is full of educated derelicts.
Persistence and determination alone are omnipotent.
The slogan Press On! has solved and always will solve the problems of the human race.
-Calvin Coolidge

In order to understand how I got to Wall Street, let me tell you a little bit about my background. After all, it's the journey, not the destination that matters.

I was born on the large island of Kodiak, Alaska which is just southwest of Anchorage. We moved from Alaska to the family farm in Eastern New Mexico before I was two years old.

For the next 15 years, I grew up in a small town that sits on the Texas border called Texico, New Mexico. The population of Texico when I was a kid was probably around 1,000 people. Most of the community lived on farms in the surrounding area.

My family had been in the region since the early 1900s, having come from East Texas and Tennessee originally. They managed our family farm for decades and from an early age I helped out doing chores and working in the fields during school breaks.

Overall, it was a pretty normal, All-American place to grow up. Very Norman Rockwell.

Confidence

You have to have confidence to work on Wall Street. In fact, you have to have confidence to even *want* to work on Wall Street. I always participated in team sports but my confidence really started to grow when I was in the seventh grade.

I played basketball that year but I wasn't very coordinated yet. I was just a tall, gangly, seventh grader getting pimples and feeling very insecure about myself. Since I was tall, however, the basketball coaches wanted me to play on the team with the eighth and ninth graders.

I thought this was great. I got to play with some of the older guys I really looked up to and suddenly started getting noticed by some of the older girls. Things were looking up.

But again, I was still pretty uncoordinated and that would come to haunt me. At some point towards the end of the season, after happily riding the bench most of the year, I was put in the game during a rather critical moment. The coach wanted three tall guys on the floor and I was to be the third posting up from the free throw line.

I'll never forget what happened next. One of the guards passed me the ball, I turned around and squared up to the basket and literally *threw* the ball at the goal.

Not *shot* the ball at the goal, which would have been great. No, I *threw* the ball at the goal. It bounced - hard - straight off the glass into the arms of a defender and immediately the other team was racing down the floor for a fast break layup.

I was pulled out of the game a few seconds later. Everyone in the gym either felt sorry for me for being so clumsy or was mad at me for giving the ball away. Those rooting for the other team were just thankful I was so terrible.

That moment sucked. A lot.

But it made me determined to never be embarrassed in sports again. I decided then and there that I was going to get better at basketball no matter what.

How do you get to Carnegie Hall? Practice, practice, practice

Back in the mid-80s, there was a large paved blacktop about the size of a football field that separated the Texico Junior High from the Texico Elementary.

The cool thing about this blacktop was that it had four basketball hoops, one in each corner of varying heights. The smallest was about eight and half feet high, the next was slightly higher, the third higher than the other two and the last one was regulation height.

After my seventh grade basketball season ended, mercifully, track season started immediately afterwards. I never really liked it but I ran track anyway because everyone else did.

However, it was about this time that I also realized I could easily slam dunk the smallest and next largest basketball goals on the blacktop.

For an uncoordinated white kid with a vertical leap that was barely in the double digits, being able to pull off a power dunk in front of your buddies was an amazing feeling.

I liked it so much, in fact, I started leaving for school a little early to be able to play before the bell rang. There was almost always someone else there to play with.

Then, during our lunch break, I'd eat as fast as I could to hurry up and get outside to maximize the amount of time we had on the court.

Finally, after track practice later in the day, I'd stop by the blacktop on the way home and play a little more. Three times a day wasn't uncommon at all.

I did this almost every day for the rest of my seventh grade year. That summer I continued to play basketball at the blacktop almost every day. I would stay at my Great Grandma Bernie's house that was only six or seven blocks from school as often as I could.

In the late summer, football two-a-days would begin. Football in West Texas/Eastern New Mexico is a big deal, as you might have heard. People there take it very seriously. My friends and I all played which meant basketball time was a bit less than before. We were only playing hoops in the morning, afternoon and some days after football practice.

Even during football season, we were still all about basketball.

While there were lots of guys who would show up to play, the three most regular were myself, my good buddy Larry Powell and Larry's cousin Benji McDaniel who was one year younger than we were. The three of us played basketball together almost every day for almost a year.

Because we could all dunk on various goals, we started expanding the way we played to look like our favorite college or pro ball players. I remember the best move was to fake someone out and drive to the goal. Then when you went for the slam dunk, right at the top you'd yell, "Jordan!"

What I loved about this play was it was so much more natural and free-flowing than the rigid set play style we used on the school team. We got to experiment with different moves, play really aggressive and experience what it feels like to close out a big move with a slam dunk.

We also got to feel how it felt to get slammed on as well. No one liked this. Anger flared up. Fights broke out from time to time. You had to be cool.

But in retrospect, these were great lessons to learn. No teams at that level could dunk on us in a gym so nothing they could do would impress us. We knew how to keep our cool so we rarely got frustrated.

By the time my eighth grade basketball season started, I was a completely different player. I had developed a solid low-post game and my timing with Larry on guard and Benji at point guard couldn't have been tighter.

From the very first practice, we knew we had something special. In fact, this would be one of the most successfully team experiences I would ever have.

One year earlier I had embarrassed myself, this year would be quite a contrast. Larry, Benji and I were an unstoppable trio.

Our team went 15-0 that year and I set the eighth grade basketball season scoring record with 242 points. A record which stood for at least a few decades.

I've had lots of other high points in my life but I can't remember enjoying any of them nearly as much as I remember that season.

We were the definition of a good team. No jealousies, lots of camaraderie and respect, lots of competitiveness and strong wills to win. Each guy had a role to play and was happy to play his part.

The three of us, however, were the core of the team and the backbone of that perfect season. We played so well together because we knew each other so well.

Each of us always knew what the other guy was thinking. Sometimes we didn't even have to make eye contact to communicate. Due to our extensive experience training together, it was just obvious what had to be done.

Perfect harmony. It doesn't happen often in life but when it does it enhances and magnifies any success you experience, when it's done with others as a team. The feeling is so much better knowing what you accomplished was not only special but practically impossible to replicate given the unique nature of the relationships involved.

I learned a lot that year and really gained an appreciation for what it means to approach something with passion. When you combine passion with the hard work necessary to achieve great things, there is almost no limit to what you can achieve.

I now knew how to get to Carnegie Hall.

Practice, practice, practice.

Wall Street on the West Coast

Fast forward quite a few years in life and I would find myself living in Southern California after joining the US Marines and later transitioning from full-time to reserve duty. I was now attending a junior college in Orange County and living with a relative in Newport Beach.

I had been attending Orange Coast College for a few years but still had no idea what I wanted to major in. One day my uncle handed me a book about Warren Buffett. I found his story fascinating. He had a shrewd eye for good investments and was famous for his frugality, both traits I admired.

So I took note of the path he took and tried to use it as a model for my own path. Buffett had an undergraduate degree in finance, then worked for a while in his father's brokerage, then he went for his MBA, then off to a career managing money.

I'll never forget, I was sitting on the beach reading one afternoon about this man and the very next day I became a business major.

Another big influence occurred in 1995 when I came across Michael Lewis' classic book *Liar's Poker*. This was when I decided that I wanted to work on the trade floor of a large investment bank.

Not only did Michael Lewis describe the kind of macho, tough-guy culture that I thought as a former Marine would be perfect for me, he also talked about the obscene amount of money these people made.

After reading about Warren Buffett and learning about the culture of Wall Street from Michael Lewis, I was hooked and knew I had found my career path.

So from that point forward I was focused, a man on a mission. I started getting all A's in school and got involved with all of the finance organizations on campus. When I finished my undergraduate degree in finance from California State University at Long Beach, I was awarded the Outstanding Finance Student Award and the Golden Nugget Leadership Award.

But the biggest opportunity I would ever get happened in the beginning of my last semester and wasn't a part of anything at school.

I was parking cars to help pay for school at The Ritz Restaurant in Fashion Island in Newport Beach, California.

This was perhaps one of the best and most productive jobs I had from a networking perspective in my entire life.

So you can picture how I looked decked out in my white dress shirt with a black bow tie, black vest, sharp black pants and all-black sneakers. Clean cut, no facial hair. No surfer dude. Just yes sir, no sir, yes ma'am, no ma'am with a smile on my face.

The owner was an Austrian and also a local legend named Hans Prager who ran a tight ship with military precision. I really liked the way he did things.

But it was hard work. We had to polish the brass poles in the front of the building every day. We parked millions of dollars' worth of exotic vehicles every day and were expected to never get a scratch. All of this in front of some of the most demanding (and condescending) customers in Newport Beach.

And yes, the tips were amazing. Around Christmas time it was particularly great. It wasn't uncommon at all for tips of $10 or $20 to be dropped. We'd take some of the local guys (those who spent a lot of money) home in Mr. Prager's limousine. These were highly coveted jobs as the customers would often leave hundreds of dollars to be split amongst us.

My buddies and I would take the little red valet tickets, use it to identify the keys and then sprint off to fetch a Mercedes or Lexus or BMW or Rolls Royce or Ferrari or, well, you get the idea.

Here's what could happen if you were paying attention to the opportunities walking in and out of that fancy restaurant each night.

"It's Hyun-dai, like *day*. We never say die."

It was spring in 1997 and I was in my junior year of college, hoping to find a good summer internship in finance to boost my chances of interviewing for investment banking jobs next year.

One night an Asian gentleman and his wife leave the restaurant and he handed me his ticket. I ran out and got in his car. After you've been a valet in a fancy parking lot for a while, you can almost instantly identify any car you sit inside even if you didn't know the make before you sat down.

You start to realize how all Ford models look like this, Mercedes always has that, Saab's are like this, Lexus like that and so forth.

However, when I got inside this gentleman's car, I was flummoxed. It looked like the interior of an Infinity but it wasn't an Infinity. Since I was in a hurry, I didn't take any time to identify the car when I was driving it up but after I arrived and opened the driver's side door. I took a few steps back and read the vehicle's name on the bumper and to my great surprise, I saw that it was a Hyundai.

It's important that I point out that by 1997 Hyundai had a pretty bad reputation in the United States. They were largely seen as cheap, poorly made vehicles.

However, this car was the opposite of that in almost every way. It was sleek, beautiful, well-appointed and easily seemed like it belonged on this lot with all the other expensive cars.

So my buddy opened the door for the wife of the gentleman and as he walked over to me I said, "This car is really nice, I can't believe it's a Hyundai. I'm actually looking to buy a car and I would never have considered a Hyundai but after driving this one I definitely would."

At this point, he unleashes a huge grin and begins to take out a business card.

Before he can get it out, I jokingly glance over to his wife and say, "Ah, is your husband a car salesman? Is he going to sell me a Hyundai?"

Instead of smiling or laughing at my joke, she looked a bit surprised and said, "Oh no, my husband is not a car salesman."

I thought I might have overstepped the bounds of valet-customer chit chat. But the gentleman kept smiling and handed me his card.

He then grabbed me by the arm and said, "It's Hyundai like day. We never say die. Get in touch with my office." Then he got in his really nice Hyundai and drove away.

I looked down at his business card. It read, M.H. "Mark" Juhn, President of Hyundai Motor America.

I thought to myself, "Jackpot."

Later that night I drafted a letter reminding him of who I was and that I was indeed looking to buy a car and if he had any good deals to offer I would consider them. I told him I was a finance major looking for a summer internship and if they had anything at Hyundai, I'd love to hear about it.

A week later I received a phone call from the President's office at Hyundai. They had a financial analyst who had recently resigned. While they were looking for her replacement, would I be interested in filling in as an extra pair of hands for the finance department over the summer.

And this was how I landed my first job in finance or Corporate America.

I got to report directly to the CFO and wrote an analysis on Volkswagen's New Beetle which was just being launched. I also did a report on their use of open versus closed auctions to sell cars they bought back from rental companies each year.

This was an amazing experience that taught me so much about corporate finance, multi-cultural workplace environments and working on a team. All because of a conversation with a customer.

I learned a great lesson that night, never stop networking. Your next big break could be the next time you tell someone you've never met before, "Hello."

The Big League

It was late 90s and money was thick in the air in Orange County and Newport Beach especially. The dotcom bubble hadn't burst yet and everyone was getting dotcom rich.

Real estate was hot as well as financing options were growing which was allowing more and more people to take out a mortgage and become homeowners.

In any case, there I was one night in late January, 1998 and two couples came out of the restaurant. There were three of us taking tickets so my two buddies grabbed theirs while I waited at the ticket booth.

While I was waiting, I overheard a gentleman lean over to his buddy and say, "I should take you upstairs and show you our new trading floor."

I immediately thought to myself, "This guy must work at PIMCO."

I knew a little about PIMCO for two reasons. First, because their headquarters was in one of the office towers above the Ritz Restaurant.

Second, due to my awareness and later research on the firm, I came to own and read a copy of legendary fixed income investor and one of PIMCO's three founders, Bill Gross' book *Everything You've Heard About Investing Is Wrong! : How to Profit in the Coming Post-Bull Markets*.

I knew this was one of those moments where fate was knocking on my door and I had to answer. Fortunately for me, the other gentleman's car arrived first and he and his wife got in and drove off. I then started chatting to the gentleman who was still waiting.

I said, "Pardon me, but I overheard you say 'trade floor,' do you happen to work at PIMCO?"

The gentleman had quite a shocked look on his face and he said to me, "I do. What do you know about PIMCO?"

I responded, "I've just finished reading Bill Gross's book. Additionally, I'm a finance major at Cal State Long Beach where I'm also the president of the Financial Management Association. We'd love to have someone from PIMCO come speak for our group."

He responded, "Hmm, maybe."

His car was getting close, I had to act.

I stepped up my game, "I graduate next May so I'm looking for any internships or part-time jobs you might have open in the firm. Can I get a business card from you and follow up with my resume?"

He smiled and pulled out a business card and handed it to me. I thanked him and tucked the card into my shirt pocket. Turned around and immediately headed out to pick up a Mercedes Benz for a local.

Later that night, I wrote a nice letter to the gentlemen reminding him about wanting someone from PIMCO to speak at CSULB. I also asked him to please keep me in mind should he have any openings become available.

About a week later I received a phone call from an assistant at PIMCO asking me to come in to their offices the next afternoon to meet my new boss Rich Tyson.

You see, the man I met that evening parking cars was Jim Muzzy, one of the other founders of PIMCO. When a part-time job opened up scanning trade tickets for the portfolio managers, he made sure I got the call.

And of course, I accepted the offer. I remember Rich walked into PIMCO's conference room where I was waiting and looked at me sort of suspiciously. Rich was an old-school Solomon Brothers guy and even back then was a very senior, intimidating type.

Rich looked at me and said, "I don't know who you are, but I'm supposed to hire you so I hope I like you."

I smiled and said, "Well, how am I doing so far?"

He smiled back and seemed to relax.

I was in.

The next thing you know I'm scanning the legendary Bill Gross's trade tickets. One day I timidly asked his trade assistant Cathy Rowe to ask him to sign my copy of his book. He did, writing, "Buy Bonds. Bill Gross."

Imagine that, one of the Gods of fixed income and a living Wall Street legend signing my book while I learned the investment management business on his trade floor.

It was amazing. And the lesson learned was the same as before. Never stop networking.

And that's how I landed my first job on Wall Street.

Introduction

> *You have not lived today until you have done something for someone who can never repay you.*
> —John Bunyan

Why write yet another book on interview skills? If you look on amazon.com there are dozens of good books on the subject already.

When I started researching investment banking and Wall Street back in 1994, there were a few books about Wall Street jobs that described what an analyst would be doing if you were working in corporate finance, sales & trading or research.

In the pre-Internet days, I found these books extremely helpful as they helped someone like me, a complete outsider, understand the basic structure of most firms and even introduced me to some industry jargon.

When it came to preparing for the actual interview, however, I found I was really out of my league. The counselors at my university had no experience with investment banking programs and had never heard of a Super Saturday.

These are the huge interview sessions organized by the investment banks where they bring in dozens of candidates who are interviewed multiple times during the day. If you've never heard of a Super Saturday, then you probably don't much about investment banking recruiting.

Besides that, the culture of investment banking was based in New York City, a place I had only seen on TV and movies. My impression of New York City was as a tough, dangerous, extremely expensive place only the bravest of souls would dare to inhabit. Therefore, I was certain that investment bankers had to be smart, tough, hardworking individuals.

But how do you prepare for a culture like that when you're a redneck from a trailer house in Eastern New Mexico whose only real world experience has been some time in the US Marines?

My answer at the time was trial and error. I read and prepared as much as I could and tried to learn something from each engagement I had. In general, this worked, but it was a long and painful way to polish my presentation.

I gained a tremendous amount of experience in this area when I was in Credit Default Sales at Deutsche Bank. In addition to my responsibilities on the trade floor, I was also in charge of the firm's MBA recruiting efforts at NYU Stern. During these four years I interviewed hundreds of candidates and saw the entire process from start to finish.

Then in 2015 I was asked to teach a communications course at Fordham University's Gabelli School of Business in their Masters of Science in Quantitative Finance program. I was given two courses with approximately 20 students each and every one of them was from China and spoke limited English at best. In addition to the generic communication skills you'd expect me to teach, the administrators of the program also wanted me to focus on improving their interview skills.

These were students that were going to be competing with other quantitative finance students from schools like MIT, Wharton and the University of Chicago. They were going to need all the help they could get. This was going to be a challenge to say the least.

So I set out to design a way to teach these students not only how to have more confidence and improve their overall communications, but to also help them focus on interview skills.

The result of this thinking is the 3x3 Interview Prep Method (3x3).

I think the 3x3 is a great way to thoughtfully and systematically prepare for the behavioral portion of the interview which should be the majority of your interview time.

Most students spend a lot of their time focused on quantitative questions only to be disappointed when they are only asked one or two. If you're unprepared to have a memorable behavioral interview, you're unprepared to interview.

The 3x3 helps you focus on exactly what you're going to say and remember it well. This allows you to demonstrate the specific traits you'll need to be considered a good candidate for the job.

Once you know the content of what you're going to say, we're then going to work on how you say it, your delivery: voice, facial expressions and eye contact, seated position, hand gestures, hand shake and more.

There's a bit more to it than that but that's essentially it. The rest is up to you and your desire to want to improve. One of my favorite expressions is, "You know how to get to Carnegie Hall? Practice, practice, practice."

I've designed this book to be accessible to anyone looking to improve their interview skills for a standard professional 30 minute to one hour interview.

I would also hope that MBA students, undergrad business students or any major looking to work on Wall Street will find value in these lessons.

I hope you find these techniques useful and I look forward to hearing your feedback on how this book has impacted your interviewing style and most importantly, the number of job offers you receive.

Part 1
Overview of the 3x3 Method

The secret of Happiness is Freedom, and the secret of Freedom, Courage.
-Thucydides, Greek Historian

If you ask an investment banking recruiter about the one thing they look for in a candidate, almost all of them will say they want to see passion. Passion for finance, passion for economics, passion for math, for computers, singing, athletics, classic cars, or even origami – almost anything can suffice. But they want to know you have the ability to be passionate about something.

But can you prepare to be passionate? Is it possible to devise and practice a strategy designed to make you look more passionate?

I believe the answer to both questions is a resounding yes.

During my professional career of over 20 years, I have interviewed thousands of people for a wide variety of jobs and opportunities. These people have come from all manner of backgrounds – some were rough and tough US Marines who only had a high school diploma when I was in the military and others were Ivy League educated all-stars when I was in investment banking.

Because of this breadth of experience, I'm often asked if there is something that I always look for or some consistent way of evaluating talent.

Just like most professional recruiters, I look for passion. I love to meet people who really convey excitement about what they want to do and have a track record of success to back up their enthusiasm.

You never know how an employee is going to work out when you first hire them so all things being equal, I'd rather hire someone with passion and give myself the optionality of above average returns on my human capital investment.

But simply saying I look for passion is easy and even a bit cliché – what employer says otherwise these days?

So is there a way I can help people prepare for their interviews that will help them seem more passionate?

Yes there is and I call it the 3x3 Method.

What is the 3x3 Method?

When you think about the structure of most interviews, you realize that there are three major topics that get discussed the most: the company, the job and the applicant.

Of course, many other things may come up during the course of the interview, but these are the big three where the majority of time is typically spent.

I don't believe in spending an inordinate amount of time preparing for a technical interview. There are some technical details you should be aware of for any job you're seeking on Wall Street but unless you're very experienced in this area already, you're not likely to get asked too many technical questions.

In my experience, most Wall Street interviews, if they are going to ask any technical questions at all, usually do so during the first few minutes of the interview. Furthermore, they typically ask no more than three and usually these questions are asked and answered rather quickly with little time spent on discussing technical details.

Most financial services firms have training programs that will teach you all you need to know when you start. Sure, they may need to know you have a certain quantitative ability or a certain level of accounting knowledge, but most firms are just looking for smart, hard-working, passionate people.

This means that your interview is likely to be overwhelmingly behavioral in nature. The vast majority of your conversation with the interviewer will be focused on the company, the job and of course, you, the candidate.

Knowing this, I want to do everything I can to prepare for these three areas in advance. The more prepared you are for what's likely to make up a majority of the conversation, the more you can relax and let your true confidence show.

To accomplish this, I want you to know at least three things about the company, the top three skills needed to perform the job and the top three skills you bring to the table.

We're also going to think about the entire process in three major areas: content, presentation and preparation.

The next few chapters focus on content. How to think about what questions you are very likely to be asked in any interview and how to strategically prepare for them.

Then we'll start focusing on your presentation. Here we'll do a deep dive into verbal and non-verbal cues.

Finally, the last few chapters talk about preparation. We'll talk about how to practice using mock interviews or your phone's video camera. We'll also discuss technical questions, your elevator pitch and how to effectively land great informational interviews.

3x3 Interview Prep Method

3 things about the company

+

3 top skills needed for the job

+

3 strong traits about yourself

+

Stories that make your experience pop

+

Excellent verbal and non-verbal delivery

+

Appropriate, professional attire

+

Confidence, good manners, excellent follow-up

+

Practice, practice, practice

=

Wall Street Dream Job

Chapter 1
The Company

> *I look for two things when I hire a new employee: ambition and humility. Without a proven track record of initiative and ambition, it's likely the person becomes a drain rather than a contributor to the company – even the really smart, talented ones.*
> *– Justin McLeod, Founder, CEO, Hinge*

How much do you know about the company with whom you're interviewing? If the head of human resources or the CEO walked in to the room and asked you to tell them about their company, could you? And if so, how much do you know?

Most companies are like tribes of people with a similar mindset all working towards a common goal. In order to join one of these tribes, the tribe members want to know that you really want to join. They want to know that you are curious about them, intrigued and impressed by what they do. Most of all, they want to know that you want to be one of them.

However, it's easy to say you want to be a part of their tribe. It's quite another thing to demonstrate through your accumulated knowledge that you've really done your homework and truly understand them.

So naturally, anyone with this desire would have done their homework. You'd have to do this before you'd have any idea about liking the tribe in the first place. This homework is going to teach you all kinds of things about the company and the people who work there.

If I'm the head of human resources and I ask you what you know about my company, I want you to tell me about the latest news, what's been happening with the stock price, who the CEO is and all the people in my firm you have already met.

I want to hear enthusiasm in your voice when you're talking about my firm because you recognize the potential opportunity it means to you. I want you to know your details because when you work for me you'll be telling others about my company and I want that pitch to be even better than this one.

I want to know, beyond a shadow of any doubt that you know about my firm and genuinely want to work there. Once I'm certain of that, then we can consider initiating you into the tribe.

Got it?

Ok, let's get started.

Go online and do some research about the company and its products. Do a news search and see if the company has been in the press recently. Visit the company's website and read about their different divisions, their history, current management, etc.

Go to Glassdoor.com and see if the company has a profile there and read some of the reviews. While they may not all be helpful (I've read some poorly written and terribly presented reviews at Glassdoor) if you read enough, a pattern will emerge.

After spending some time researching the company, make sure you know at least three major things about the firm. Exactly what these things are will vary from firm to firm so you'll need to understand what's most important.

Perhaps the CEO is a public figure. If so, you should probably know a little about him or her. Or maybe the company has been in the news lately for a major success or scandal. That's important to know too.

Definitely know a little bit about the company's size in terms of revenue and geographic footprint. Know about their competitors and how the company is positioned in the marketplace. If you have friends or LinkedIn connections who work or used to work at the firm, reach out to them and try to find out as much about the company's culture as possible.

For most interviews, it's unlikely that you'll spend a lot of time discussing the company. But if you know at least three important things about the company, you'll be able to have a relatively comfortable discussion with the interviewer if and when the topic comes up.

Now back to passion. When I was interviewing someone and they told me a) I'm very passionate about the job but b) I know nothing about your company – I'd get suspicious.

This does not indicate passion but someone who knows what buzzwords to use. I now know that the word passion for this person is just that, a word.

If you really are going to convey passion, you've got to know more about the company than the average candidate. Know at least three major things about the company.

Understanding the Company

The People

- Current CEO
- Board members
- Current executive team – CFO, COO, CMO, Head of HR, CTO, etc.
- Heads of major product areas or teams
- Major investors

The Organization

- History and About section on company webpage
- Company milestones, major successes or failures
- Current products
- Current stock price information
- Major competitors and understanding of industry position

After reading all of the above information, be prepared to talk about at least three of them

Chapter 2
The Job

You have to learn the rules of the game. And then you have to play better than anyone else.
-Albert Einstein

This is where things start to get interesting and personal. How well do you really know the role you're trying to land? Do you understand the culture of the firm at which you'll be working and how that can affect the role?

Most jobs have a certain set of skills that are required to be able to successfully perform the function. These can be general things like tenacity, attention to detail, ability to handle stress, ability to work long hours, people skills, etc. Other times the skills could be highly specific like knowledge of a certain computer programming language, particular math or quantitative skills or knowledge of a particular client or industry.

Try to think from the perspective of the employer. What would be the top three skills they'd like to see in someone to be able to do the job well? Your odds of getting any job go way up when you can successfully demonstrate that you have the major tools needed to get the job done at a high level.

Once you've identified the three things you think are most critical to getting the job done well, (from the perspective of the employer) then you're ready to start thinking about yourself.

Understanding the Job

People Skills

- Demonstrated team player
- Hard working, understand the long hours involved
- Experience managing people, leadership skills
- Experience dealing with stress, thick skinned, not easily rattled
- Attention to detail, organized, punctual
- Competitive, know how to win
- Intellectual curiosity, desire to learn more about finance
- Embraces failure and learns from it
- Self-motivated, self-disciplined

Technical Skills

- Understanding of accounting, balance sheets, financial statements
- Understanding of quantitative math, advanced computer programming languages
- Understanding of economics and global markets
- Previous experience working in finance or investment banking, knowledge of a trade floor or investment banking group
- Understanding of industry players – 40 Act mutual funds, hedge fund, PE funds, family offices, pensions, foundations, endowments and others

> The list above is not exhaustive, there are many other people or technical skills you may want to discuss. Think about the role and the firm and decide what you think are the three most important skills the company expects you to have for the role you want.

Chapter 3
The Candidate

> *I prefer to win titles with the team ahead of individual awards or scoring more goals than anyone else. I'm more worried about being a good person than being the best football player in the world. When all this is over, what are you left with? When I retire, I hope I am remembered for being a decent guy.*
> *-Lionel Messi, Argentina's greatest soccer star*

Think about the three top skills that you bring to the table. Of course you're going to have more than three skills that you think are important but the interview typically only lasts 45-minutes to an hour, you don't have time to go through your entire biography, pick your top three and go with that.

Spoiler alert – you may have figured this out already but the three skills you choose to highlight about yourself should be highly correlated if not exactly the same as the three top skills needed to perform the job well.

See how that works? Understanding what skills make for a successful employee in that role should help you determine what skills of your own to highlight.

If you've taken the time to really think about what you want to do and have chosen a career on Wall Street because you feel it is a good match for your skillset – hard worker, likes solving financial puzzles, good with math, enjoys economics, likes researching companies, etc. – then you'll be fine.

If you're choosing a career on Wall Street because the pay is very high, well, the 3x3 will still help you get a job but you might find that Wall Street isn't all you thought it could be.

The hours can be grueling. The work can be very technical and complicated. Your coworkers can be intense, competitive types willing to play politics to move ahead. Not knowing what you're getting in to can mean a bad fit you might regret for years.

But let's assume you know what you're doing, have thought about the job you want and know how your own strengths match up with the job requirements. Here are a few of the big ones that work well in almost any investment banking interview.

People and communication skills

Investment bankers talk to a lot of people with their own particular language. You'll need to be fluent in your ability to speak to senior bankers, traders, hedge fund portfolio managers, CEOs, CFOs, investor relations personnel, technology providers, academics, coworkers, junior employees, restaurant and bar staff, Uber car drivers, hotel staff, sommeliers, tailors and others.

Sales skills

From the second you arrive on Wall Street you will be in sales mode. Maybe not selling a product per se, but you're always going to be selling (or trying to convince people) about ideas, concepts, products, companies, models, strategies, methodologies, etc. The stronger your sales skills, the greater your success on Wall Street.

Trading or valuation skills

The ability to recognize an asset that is mispriced is fundamental to the banking and investing business. Anything you've done in the past that had to do with trading or valuing any kind of product or service should be mentioned.

Quantitative and/or programming skills

Any experience programming using Visual Basic in Excel, modeling using advanced math or programming languages like C++ Visual Basic, Python, MATLAB and others is extremely valued. Block chain is happening now along with things like artificial intelligence, high frequency trading, robo-advisors and lots of other financial technology innovations. The more math and programming, the better.

Work ethic

In case you weren't aware by now, don't choose a career on Wall Street because of the flexible hours and work life balance (whatever that means). Any of the times in your life when you've put in the long hours and really been the work horse for your team should be discussed. They're absolutely looking for this characteristic.

Intellectual curiosity

What is your thirst for new knowledge like? Do you get excited when you learn a new formula or gain important knowledge about a market? How many books on the market have you read? How many books on the market are you reading? What clubs or hobbies are you involved with that further bolsters your quest for knowledge. Most folks on Wall Street are smart and crave knowledge.

Think hard about everything you've done and how those experiences could fit one of the categories above. Now start to think about how you'd tell the story of that experience in a meaningful way.

This brings us to the next section. Now we're going to take the traits you want to highlight and pair them with your own experience to craft a memorable story.

Good stories highlighting a solid track record are memorable and score exactly the kind of interview points you want to score.

Chapter 4
Understanding the Candidate: Story Development for Each Bullet

I emphasize to C.E.O.s, you have to have a story in the minds of the employees. It's hard to memorize objectives, but it's easy to remember a story.
-Ben Horowitz

Now we get down to the hard part – converting this knowledge about the skills needed for the job and the skills you bring to the table into a powerful interview. To accomplish this, we need to be prepared to talk about anything on our resume.

The trick here though is not to simply restate what's written on your resume when the interviewer says, "Tell me about your time at Company X." Restating what's written on your resume doesn't introduce anything new or help the interviewer understand you in a way she doesn't already.

Instead, we want to look at every major component of our resume and come up with meaningful stories that tell what we did at that job or experience.

This is a great way to build interest in your background and make the interview more memorable, as stories resonate in our memory much longer than just boring facts and figures.

The stories should highlight aspects from your past that clearly demonstrate you already have the kind of stuff needed to be a success.

However, the stories you're going to develop aren't random. They are linked to the top three skills about the job and yourself that you decided on earlier.

Building stories

Let's say that you were applying for an entry-level investment banking analyst role. Further, you had decided that the skills most needed for this role are a strong work ethic, ability to handle stress and solid attention to detail.

Then, once you decide what stories you could tell about the major parts of your resume, you'll craft each story's theme to be one of strong work ethic, ability to handle stress and/or solid attention to detail. You can focus on one skill per story or combine multiple skills into the same story.

What starts to happen is that each time the interviewer asks you about a certain part of your resume, you respond with an interesting, engaging story that ultimately ends with you highlighting how in that previous experience you were already doing the things you'd need to be doing for the job you want.

For example, our inspiring investment banker wants to highlight her strong work ethic and is asked about her role as the president of her sorority in college. Her response should tell a story about a time when she really had to work long hours and be incredibly focused to pull things together under a tight timeline and still kept the rest of her life in order.

She might say something like, "My time as the president of my sorority was one of my best experiences in college. I'll never forget how much time and effort it took for us to organize our final ball. We worked in multiple shifts for weeks to get all the details done but we all bonded through this process and became much tighter as a team. That my sorority also maintained the highest GPA average of all the other organizations was something we were all proud of."

As she's telling this story, hopefully the interviewer is thinking, "Wow, she organized the efforts of multiple people to pull off a successful event, bonded with her team and still maintained her discipline on grades. That's the kind of work ethic and teamwork we need here."

Now the next question she's asked is about an internship she had at a local bank. "So tell me about your role at Community Federal Savings," the interviewer might ask.

"Sure," she would respond. "That was a really great summer experience last year. I was working with the head of commercial loan origination to identify new targets for their new industrial rate loans. There was a period during July where I worked long hours with my boss to build an algorithm that would identify suitable targets from a database of firms in the Pacific Northwest. Then, after helping him organize the target companies into an organized spreadsheet, I spent two weeks calling dozens of CFOs pitching our expertise. I learned so much on that project."

Can you see how much more effective it is to answer these questions with stories that bring real world examples out? It makes you more memorable as a candidate and helps the interviewer understand how good of a fit you might potentially be.

Practice your stories

The more you practice saying these stories out loud, the better you'll get at presenting them in an interview.

You'll also realize that some stories you're using are too long, or aren't specific enough, or leave key details out. So try it again and change some things. Then do it again, and again - rinse, wash, repeat.

After you've practiced these stories out loud 10-20 times, you'll really know what you want to say and how you want to say it.

Knowing in advance what skills you want to highlight and the stories you'll use to highlight them in the best possible way allows you the freedom during the interview to really focus on your verbal and non-verbal cues to build a passionate presence.

A passionate presence combined with a strong knowledge of the company and a background filled with relevant experience adds up to a candidate with a great chance of landing the job.

Stories, not statements

Consider the words of the ancient Roman philosopher Epictetus who expresses the need to be able to show your strengths by actions (stories) rather than just declarations.

Simply saying you're smart, or experienced or hard working isn't enough. Demonstrate to me, through the stories of things you've done, that you are indeed a worthy candidate.

"Don't declare yourself to be a wise person or discuss your spiritual aspirations with people who won't appreciate them. Show your character and commitment to personal nobility through your actions."

-Epictetus (circa 55-135 CE)

Resume Story Development Example

3 Skills Chosen to Highlight

1. Accounting, operations and financial knowledge

2. Hard working, understand how to make money

3. Strong quantitative academic background

The skills above are typical for most research, sales & trading and corporate finance jobs. There are dozens of other skills you might list above these three for any particular role or firm, but let's use these as an example.

Once you've established the three you want to focus on, let's go to your resume. First off, if you have more than a one-page resume, you are wrong. Edit it and design a nice one-pager. No one needs a two-page resume, especially someone relatively junior.

Next, you'll want to think about each job or experience on your resume as a chance to highlight one of the skills above with an interesting story. Bear in mind this is going to be completely different than what the bullet points say on your resume.

For example, you may have a bullet point on your resume like this under a previous internship you had at a small mutual fund:

- Responsible for overseeing the fund's daily cash reconciliation

This is a very interesting bullet point and likely to catch an interviewer's eye. However, what you don't want to do is simply regurgitate the bullet point if asked about this job. Here's how this exchange typically goes:

Interviewer: "So tell me about your experience at XYZ Bank, it looks like you were involved with the administration of one of their funds, tell me about that?"

Your answer: "Yes, each day I was responsible for making sure any cash balance left in the fund after all the day's buys and sells was invested in short-term securities to maximize the fund's return."

While the answer given is technically correct, it fails because all you've really done is rehash what you said in the bullet point in a slightly different way. Again, the answer isn't wrong, just boring as hell, unmemorable and adds little to your case to get hired.

Instead, come up with a story about the job that not only tells what you were doing but also highlights one or all of the three skills you want to highlight.

A story like this for example, "Yes, I was a part of the team that invested remaining cash balances at the end of the day. For example, I used to monitor the daily investments of our commercial paper trader and noticed that he often left balances of greater than $500k in some accounts.

I asked him if I could move the rest of the cash into AAA-rated short-term municipal variable rate notes and he approved. The ability to buy short-term paper in small lot sizes meant the cash balance was maximized to the specifications of the client and the extra yield generated thousands of dollars in extra income and a few basis points in performance over the next few months."

In this way, you demonstrate a few key skills by working with other executives, connecting financial markets and problem solving in the financial markets. All good points to score.

And if you're lucky, maybe you've hit a nerve with the interviewer and he or she will remember your story. Maybe they had a similar job when they were junior and could really relate to your experience.

Make the story memorable. You are the star one way or another, even if you're describing a failure or giving someone else credit, you're still demonstrating skills they might want to see.

See the example on the next page for an overview of how to think about your resume. Each section is an opportunity to come up with one or a few really great stories that highlight at least your three strongest traits.

Don't overlook the bottom section that usually discusses your other interests. I think this is a great spot on the resume to add interesting or unusual facts about you that can be turned into great stories.

For example, one bullet point that I have used since my MBA days at NYU Stern is the PADI-certified Rescue SCUBA Diver certification I hold. This allows me to tell some great stories about diving and ocean rescues that really make the interview interesting and memorable for a few minutes. It also allows me to highlight my attention to risk management which is always critical for any job in finance.

I also have a section which discusses my basic language skills in Spanish and Portuguese. This allows me to highlight skills and show some humility at the same time. It's great to be confident, it's also great when people admit they don't know it all and are eager to learn.

Build Stories That Highlight Your Three Skills

BRIAN A. ROGERS
Rose Hill, New York, NY 10010
917-123-4567 brian.rogers@rogersgroupnyc.net
http://www.linkedin.com/in/brianarogers

Experience 2013-present	**THE ROGERS GROUP** Principal/Founder • Communication expert focused on improving the investor communication skills of C-level executives • Creator of the 3x3 Method for improving interview skills, soon to be a textbook	New York, NY
2012-present	**NEW YORK UNIVERSITY, LEONARD N. STERN SCHOOL OF BUSINESS** Adjunct Professor – Business Communication for the Langone MBA Program	New York, NY
2015-present	**FORDHAM UNIVERSITY, GABELLI SCHOOL OF BUSINESS** Adjunct Professor – Business Communication for the Master of Science in Quantitative Finance Program	New York, NY
2014-2016	**MARKETS GROUP** Head of Human Resources, Training and Development • One of three key executives in charge of overall company direction and strategy • Served as the Head of Marketing, the Head of the Credit and Hedge Funds Group and the Head of the Private Wealth Latin America Group	New York, NY
2012-2013	**ESPIRITO SANTO INVESTMENT BANK** Executive Director • Brazil, India and Poland equity research sales for US-based emerging markets investors	New York, NY
2010-2011	**FATOR SECURITIES, LLC.** Head of International Equity Research Sales • Implemented strategy to develop institutional equity research sales business in the US, UK and Europe	New York, NY
2008-2010	**SAFRA SECURITIES CORPORATION** Head of International Equity Research Sales • One of original team members hired to develop the international capital markets business for Banco Safra	New York, NY
2004-2008	**DEUTSCHE BANK SECURITIES, INC.** Structured Credit Derivative Sales • Executed credit default swaps on structured products including CDOs	New York, NY
1998-2002	**PACIFIC INVESTMENT MANAGEMENT COMPANY (PIMCO)** Portfolio Associate • Fixed income execution trader overseeing trades for multiple portfolio managers	Newport Beach, CA
1990-1998	**UNITED STATES MARINE CORPS, 3RD ANGLICO** Forward Air Controller & Humvee Mechanic	Long Beach, CA
Academic 2004	**NEW YORK UNIVERSITY, LEONARD N. STERN SCHOOL OF BUSINESS** Master of Business Administration, Emphasis in Economics and Financial Instruments	New York, NY
1998	**CALIFORNIA STATE UNIVERSITY, COLLEGE OF BUSINESS ADMINISTRATION** Bachelor of Science in Business Administration, Emphasis in Finance, magna cum laude	Long Beach, CA
Additional	• Proficient in Spanish and basic understanding of Portuguese • Yoga to the People certified Hot Yoga Instructor • PADI certified Rescue SCUBA Diver	

Stories about entrepreneurial work, creativity, public speaking

Stories about leadership, team work, team player

Stories about technical skills and market experience

General success and humorous stories meant to make a lasting impression

Chapter 5
Develop an Elevator Pitch

The purpose of an elevator pitch is to describe a situation or solution so compelling that the person you're with wants to hear more even after the elevator ride is over.

-Seth Godin

Let's take stock of what we've been doing thus far. We've put a lot of time into thinking about the companies and industry in which we want to work and how our own story fits the narrative of those already in the business.

Then we did a deep dive into our resume and came up with compelling stories for each major section.

Now is a perfect time to think about and develop a good elevator pitch. Why? Why not. It's something that you'll be using for the rest of your career. Take this opportunity and use the momentum you've built to develop this key bit of branding about yourself.

A lot of people work on this in MBA programs but if you've never developed one, let's do it now.

In order to get these interviews, you will need to be emailing, phoning and meeting with people all the time and you'll need a good elevator pitch for introduction purposes.

But the time you'll need it the most is that awkward moment when someone really important starts chatting with you and says, "So, tell me what brings you here?"

The first thing is to realize that there is no exact time length for a good elevator pitch but in general it should be short. I suggest working on a least a couple different lengths. A short version of about 30-45 seconds and a long version of 1:30 to two minutes.

Do it now while these stories are fresh

Why is this so important? Think of your elevator pitch as more than just a brief historical walk in your past. If you tell the story properly, it explains a little bit about who you are and why doing what you're doing now makes so much sense.

Even in the short version, you want to leave your audience with a positive opinion about where you are on your journey.

An elevator pitch should summarize where you've been, what you did and how that has brought you to your current objective. Similar to a company's mission statement, it's your big picture description that helps people understand who you are and where you want to go.

A few important items first, **a) don't lie or over-exaggerate.** Hopefully this encounter could lead to an interview where they will be reviewing your background and perhaps even doing a professional background check. Make sure you stick to the facts and match what's on your resume. And **b) make it memorable.**

Another thing to consider, where you start your elevator pitch depends on where you are in your career. If you're a bit more senior and have a few years of business experience, perhaps you don't even need to mention your undergraduate or MBA program.

Instead, start at the beginning of your professional career and work up.

Another exception might be if you had something particularly unique from your youth like a major success in athletics or major academic achievements.

These stories are great because they provide a window into not only how you got to where you are today but they also reveal very important aspects about your self-discipline, work ethic and intelligence.

Elevator Pitch
Basic Structure

Experience A
- Helped me understand fixed income market
- Developed quant skills

Experience B
- Provided valuable leadership experience
- Taught me how to implement strategy
- Worked extremely long hours

Experience C
- Worked with senior managers
- Allowed me to focus on developing investor relationships

That's why I'm here today

Part 2
Maximizing Your Presence

Your hand opens and closes, opens and closes. If it were always a fist or always stretched open, you would be paralysed. Your deepest presence is in every small contracting and expanding, the two as beautifully balanced and coordinated as birds' wings.
-Jalaluddin Rumi, The Essential Rumi

There is this thing that we all have, that never leaves us and is always recognizable by others. We call it presence. But you can also think of it as your aura, your energy, your glow, your chi, how you radiate...

While almost all of us want to show up to our next interview with our best presence, we're not always able to do that.

So I'd like to spend some time talking about presence and specifically where your presence lives – in the combination of your verbal and non-verbal gestures.

By understanding how to use your body and voice to their maximum effect and then practicing those skills consistently, you can begin to build a powerful presence.

After years of teaching executives how to become better speakers, I've noticed a few common mistakes that many people make that are easy to fix.

The idea here is to understand how your presence is always a part of us, no matter where we are or what we're doing. The following tips are designed for all types of presentation situations including times when you're standing and times when you're seated as you will be for most interviews.

All of these things can be practiced regularly around your home, school or office and I recommend that you do exactly that.

Tip #1 – More smile and consistent eye contact

Your audience, whether it's one person in an interview or 50 people in a presentation, do not want you to fail, they want you to succeed. They are hoping your presentation is engaging and entertaining because, after all, we all like to be entertained, hear great stories and meet great people. So you have to know from the beginning that the audience is on your side.

But how do you keep them there?

The easiest and best thing you can do is to simply smile a bit more often and make good eye contact. Don't overestimate the simple effectiveness of a smile and the acknowledgement you give someone when you make eye contact with them.

If you're speaking in front of a larger audience, good eye contact should be a slow scanning motion that neither goes too fast nor too slow. Don't look up or down too much and don't focus on one person for too long.

For the seated interview, you should maintain good eye contact about 70% of the time. Break occasionally as you think about things but generally maintain attentive eye contact.

The smile should be used whenever appropriate. During much of the conversation in an interview you won't be smiling but actively listening. However, when an opportunity comes to smile and lighten the mood, always do it.

A big smile and consistent eye contact are very powerful tools, use them.

Tip #2 – Too many or not enough hand gestures

Hand gesture issues come in two varieties – too many or not enough. If you're one of those people like me who has always identified as someone who talks a lot with your hands, you're probably using them too much.

We'll talk more specifically about hand gestures in an upcoming section but a good way to check yours is by getting out your trusty video camera and recording yourself delivering one of the stories you've been developing. Notice if your hands are adding emphasis to specific words at specific points in time or if they are simply in constant motion.

Adding emphasis at the right times is good, constant motion is bad. Constant motion becomes like background white noise to the audience – it's always there, never stops and quickly becomes annoying.

Edit these gestures by bringing your hands back down to your sides occasionally and delivering a few words while not moving them.

On the other hand, if you're not moving your hands at all, try to make more effort to use them. Try to coordinate your movements to specific parts of your story to help make your meaning more clear.

A few good hand gestures can really go a long way.

Tip #3 – Awkward stance, fidgety legs and feet

Speakers often give away their nervousness by the way they stand. Even if your eye contact and smile are good and your voice is confident, if you are tapping your foot, standing awkwardly with one foot in front of the other or hip-sitting, you will appear nervous or simply less confident to the audience.

The good thing about a bad stance is that it's a relatively easy thing to clean up. Allow me to introduce you to the natural/neutral position for both standing and seated presentations.

The way you set up is by getting your feet even, placed squarely under the shoulders, toes pointing directly forward. Stand up tall with your neck and spine in alignment. Relax your hands and let them hang naturally at your side. It's important that you neither clench them into a fist nor extend your fingers too straight.

Practice this position by setting up your video camera and filming another one to two-minute story. This time you want to keep your legs and feet "quiet" by not moving them and keeping them squared up and solid throughout.

It's very similar for the seated presentation during an interview. Keep your legs and feet squarely facing the interviewer to make sure your upper body is also facing forward.

Don't tap your feet or move your legs back and forth. Sit still and keep your legs quiet. Just because you're sitting down doesn't mean your legs can take a break. They still have a job to play even if that job is only to not be distracting and help you sit up straight.

Tip #4 – Voice is too monotone or volume too low

I've always thought it was helpful to think of the voice as a musical instrument. In many ways, your voice is like the spirit of your presentation. If you come out flat, monotone and soft, audiences will quickly tune out as your instrument will be boring to them.

Instead, think about your stories and where you can use your voice to its full effect. Some basic things to consider would be to get louder or softer, speak faster or slower, increase or decrease the pitch or your voice and finally, from time to time, add some emotion into your voice.

Tip #5 – No movement, like a statue

We talked about the natural/neutral above and the importance of not having lazy or twitchy feet and legs. Once you've mastered the natural/neutral, add in some movement across the stage to really keep the audience's attention.

The movement you'll be adding, however, is meaningful which is why we call it movement with a purpose (MWP). It's not just random movement for no reason, it's strategic.

What you'll do is find a natural transition in your speech as you're moving from one topic to the other and then as you get to this part, take a three or four steps to your left or right, then set up in the natural/neutral again in front of a new section of the audience.

These steps should be done calmly and in a controlled manner. Try to keep your eyes on the audience as you walk. It's really important here that you don't lose eye contact with the side of the audience you just left.

Keep making eye contact throughout the entire room even when you move to the opposite side of the room.

In addition to the side-to-side movements, you can also move towards the audience when you want to make a big point or get their attention or away from the audience when you want to deemphasize something or slow things down.

This talking and walking is harder than it sounds. Set up that video camera and record yourself. This will take more practice than most of the other items but it will really enhance your presence when you can do it well.

For the seated presentation or interview, you can accomplish a lot of the same impact of movement even while seated. While you're telling stories, you can lean slightly to the left or right, or lean slightly forward or back. This helps add or remove emphasis at key moments and makes your presentation much more visually interesting.

Tip #6 – No story structure

This is a bit redundant but it's so important it's worth repeating. One of the biggest mistakes you can make isn't actually something that comes from your verbal or non-verbal cues. It's not having a good story structure for the audience to follow.

Humans love stories. It seems like we're almost evolutionarily wired to recognize good story structure. When audiences hear good stories, they respond by being attentive, engaged and appreciative. This is exactly what we want.

However, audiences can also tell when you haven't prepared enough and thought about a good story structure. And naturally, they will tune you out and become disengaged.

To keep things simple, just think about the basic formula for writing a story – you need a beginning, middle and an end. I like to say, "Tell them what you're going to tell them; tell them; tell them what you told them."

While this sounds easy enough, many people won't grasp this and instead simply stand in front of an audience and list facts rather than telling the story of those facts. Don't fall for this trap. Present your information in a story-like manner and audiences will love you for it.

Standing or seated, both are presentations

You'll notice that in this section at other times throughout the book, I'll talk about your interview from the perspective of both a standing and seated presentation.

The reason for this is simple, while the vast majority of your actual interviews will be sitting down, you won't always be seated while you're presenting yourself to others.

Sometimes you might be asked to give a quick presentation. Other times you might be networking at a cocktail party and get questions about your resume – which would be a perfect opportunity to practice your elevator pitch and your stories.

Which is why I want to discourage you from only practicing the seated position. Also work on your standing presentation. The standing presentation is harder, there is more to think about and you are more exposed.

However, once you get good at it, you'll realize that the same skills you need for the standing presentation are exactly the same skills you need for the seated except there are less things to remember and you'll feel more confident sitting.

In the seated interview, you don't have to worry about walking around and your stance. You also don't have to walk in front of the audience. This makes the seated interview much easier than a standing presentation. Practice both and your skills will develop quickly.

Chapter 6
How to Walk into the Room with Confidence

Courage is not the absence of fear, it is the ability to act in the presence of fear.
-Bruce Lee

A recent study by the *Journal of Occupational and Organizational Psychology* showed that about 5% of the decisions were made within the first minute of the interview.

Further, about 30% had made up their mind within five minutes. Now consider a whopping 52% of the interviewers had made up their mind between five and fifteen minutes into the interview. The remaining interviewers hadn't made up their mind by the time the interview was over.

First off, in the tradition of *The Hitchhiker's Guide to the Galaxy*, don't panic. Feeling nervous before an interview is perfectly natural. In fact, you'd be pretty strange if you didn't get a little nervous.

The trick is not letting that nervousness grow too large or be visible to others. So let's talk about some tips to stay calm and cool before your next interview.

Tip #1: Find a bathroom

Seriously, go find a bathroom and do the pride pose for two minutes. This is a specific reference to Harvard Professor Amy Cuddy's Ted Talk where she describes doing the Pride Pose in the bathroom for two minutes before an important interview to feel more confident. I think this is an amazing idea, do it.

Arrive at the company five to ten minutes early and ask for the bathroom. Go into a stall and close the door. Now clench your fists and put them both straight up in the air above your head, look up and put a big smile on your face. Hold this for two minutes.

You won't regret it.

Pride Pose

- Hands clenched in a fist
- Arms up high over your head
- Eyes looking up towards the ceiling
- Big smile with teeth showing

Do this before every interview

- 2 minutes in the bathroom
- Increases testosterone – dominance hormone
- Reduces cortisol – stress hormone

Tip #2: Caffeine

Have a coffee, espresso or a chocolate bar about an hour before your interview. This should help wake you up and make you more attentive.

Caffeine effects everyone differently so be aware of your own body and if caffeine is a bad choice for you, don't do it. I also don't recommend you do this on an empty stomach. Definitely eat something before your interview.

But for many people, stopping at Starbucks or having a homemade coffee before your interview is a good thing.

Tip #3: Jam out a little bit

Listen to music that makes you feel motivated and uplifted on your way to the interview. Sing if you can, warm up your voice a little.

Tip #4: Think about your stories

Practice your answers in your head on your way to the interview. Think about the stories you've been practicing, rehearse them in your head on your way to the interview.

Tip #5: Long, calming yoga breaths

If you've ever taken a yoga class, you know how important breathing is to a healthy practice and how it helps calm you down and keep you cool.

These techniques are designed to be effective while performing a 90-minute yoga series in a room heated to 115 degrees Fahrenheit. If they can work in that environment, they can certainly work in the comfortable climate you'll find in any financial services firm.

Take four second inhales in your nose then release the breath out of your nose again, but this time for six seconds. Make these really long, slow consistent breaths in and out of your nose.

Do this ten or fifteen times. It will really slow down your breathing and your mind. If you can close your eyes, do so. If you're in public and this isn't' possible, try to relax your eyes and gaze at something a few feet away. This will really help calm your mind and body.

Tip #6: Think positive

The Power of Positive Thinking is a book written by Dr. Norman Vincent Peale back in 1952. It's a great book to read about how to develop that voice in your head that says, "I can do this," and tune out the voice that says, "You can't." I highly recommend you read this book or one like it while you're searching for a job.

It's important to recognize that if you're doing your job hunt properly you'll be applying to a lot of jobs to maximize your chance of getting at least one. But by definition this means you're likely to get a lot of No responses. Learn to see this as a good thing. Each No just gets you closer to the final Yes.

Remember, most interviewers will establish an opinion about you very quickly. Make sure from the moment you walk in the door you look and sound your absolute best. Make a strong first impression, your stories will only bolster that positive image.

Chapter 7
Four Parts of the Voice

Be a craftsman in speech that thou mayest be strong, for the strength of one is the tongue, and speech is mightier than all fighting.
                                    -Maxims of Ptahhotep, 3400 B.C.

The idea that we should be mindful of our speech in terms of both what we're going to say and how we're going to say it is a very old concept. The quote above goes all the way back to 3400 B.C. and I'm sure the concept had been around for a long time before that.

Humans communicate. That's just what we do. In fact, it's my view that this is the reason for living. It's not why we're here, I have no clue about who created us or where we're going when we die. But while we're here, our job is to communicate.

This is how we've shared information for thousands of years – communication. You've got to imagine that for vast stretches of human history, humans roamed the planet following food sources and on occasion came across other humans. I think it is far more likely that we tried hard to communicate with each other rather than trying to fight each other.

Violence was dangerous and led to injuries and sometimes death. These were terminal activities during most of human times. It made much more sense that we would see new people as potential resources and find ways to trade with one another – knowledge, skills and materials – than just mindlessly try to murder each other.

We used facial expressions, hand gestures, body language, our volume and pace, pitch/tone and occasionally loaded our voice with timbre or emotion.

And we're still doing it today, it's just much more refined and rehearsed. But the strategic use of the voice is evident in many aspects of our lives.

Listen for the music

Close your eyes and imagine yourself in the congregation of a large church in the Deep South on a Sunday afternoon listening to a really dynamic preacher give his sermon. Before I even tell you what to think about next, you're probably already imagining how colorful and creative the preacher's voice sounds.

You're imagining the way the preacher gets really loud sometimes and pounds on the pulpit to make a point. Or how she'll tell a funny story with lightness and laughter in her voice. At other points you can imagine her slowing down dramatically to let certain points land and then sometimes speeding up to add drama.

There is almost a musical characteristic to what the preacher is doing. While she's not singing, there is certainly a rhythmic nature to the sermon she's delivering. In short, she's using her voice as an instrument to deliver her message.

While most of us will never have to preach a sermon in front of a congregation, it's important to understand what the verbal tools are that great speakers use to enhance their presentation. Specifically today, I want to think about the four basic aspects of your voice: volume, tone/pitch, pace and timbre.

Most people don't know this but I used to play the trumpet when I was in high school. I used to compete in solo competitions and regularly performed with my school's jazz band. Thinking of your voice as a musical instrument is very helpful. All four parts of your voice can find their equivalent in a musical context.

Volume

This one is probably the easiest to begin with. At all points in time during your presentation, your voice should be loud enough to be heard clearly by the person in the room who is the farthest away from you.

For the seated interview, this shouldn't typically be a problem. However, if you find yourself in an interview with multiple people, make sure they can all hear you clearly.

Use your volume strategically by slowly getting louder at big points in your presentation and then sometimes speaking more softly as you change your pace.

Think of this crescendo and decrescendo – to get louder or to get softer. Modify your voice the same way an orchestra modifies its sound by getting louder at certain points and softer at others to draw emphasis to the particular music being played.

Tone/Pitch

Some people think that tone/pitch are the same thing as volume. They are similar but different at the same time. Tone/pitch can be thought of as musical notes on a scale that is going up or down. The tone/pitch of your voice, will get higher or lower depending on where the particular note is on the scale.

Notice that this doesn't necessarily mean that as your tone/pitch gets higher your volume goes up. It might, but that's a separate choice about volume. Conversely, lowering your pitch doesn't necessarily mean your volume will go down.

Imagine a singer warming up to the classic lines from the Sound of Music, "Do, re, me, fa, so, la, ti." Notice how the tone/pitch changes as the singers sings the words but the volume remains the same.

Pace

This is a really fun one to play with. Changing the pace at key moments in your presentation is something that can really draw interest to what you are saying. In musical terms we would refer to pace as tempo and we would measure this in beats per minute (same thing as with your heart rate). Musically, there are dozens of way to describe how to get faster or slower, however, here we'll keep things simple.

There are a number of good examples to use when thinking about presenters who use pace changes in an effective way but the example that always comes to me is the actor William Shatner and how he used pace changes to deliver his lines as Capt. James T. Kirk in the original Star Trek. If you don't know what I'm talking about, do a quick YouTube search and watch a few his old videos.

Shatner's use of pace changes drew attention to what he was saying. Over the years, his style of speaking has become the target of many comedians' routines, however, for the most part this is just testimony to how effective and memorable his speech was.

One of his main weapons was the dramatic pause. For example, after asking a big question or making a big statement, he'd pause for just a few seconds to let the statement really land and allow the audience to come up with their own answer before he delivers his next line.

Dramatically speeding up or slowing down your pace from its established norms is a great way to call attention back to you and grab your audience's attention.

Timbre

No, I'm not talking about a hit song from the rapper Pitbull. In music, timbre refers to the particular quality or uniqueness of a sound that differentiates it from the tone/pitch. In public speaking, I refer to timbre as the emotion you add in to your voice that is distinct from simply getting louder or changing your pitch or pace.

Think of the timbre in someone's voice who was giving a very aggressive, angry speech. Now think about the timbre that might be present in a coach's voice as she tried to rally her team to victory. Finally, think about the timbre in someone's voice who's delivering the eulogy at a funeral.

As you can imagine, all of the above have lots of emotion packed in to their delivery. You can hear it and feel it. If the speaker is really doing their job well, the addition of timbre will likely be very persuasive, inspiring you to do something or feel a particular way.

Using timbre effectively is a great way to make your message more memorable. However, one word of caution, a speech that relies on too much timbre can quickly become tiresome. The right amount of emotion can be very effective in delivering your message. Too much emotion and your presentation can be exhausting and cause audiences to tune out.

Practice, practice, practice

The best way to know if you're using your voice effectively is to record yourself delivering a speech. Set up your video or audio recorder and tape a 2-3 minute presentation and intentionally try to work on the four parts of the voice we've discussed – volume, tone/pitch, pace and timbre.

The first time you hear your own voice on a recording it's awkward, I know. It doesn't sound the way you think it should. Don't worry, you'll get used to it. That is how you sound and it's fine. Now focus on the technical details.

Notice your volume and if you're changing it. Notice your tone/pitch and how you can use it to build interest. Notice your pace and how speeding up or using dramatic pauses can wake the audience up. And finally, notice if the timbre you're using is effective and also whether you're using it enough or too much.

Think of your voice like an instrument and learn how to use yours like a seasoned musician.

Four Parts of the Voice

Volume: loud enough to be heard by the person in the room farthest away from you

Pitch/Tone: vary tone throughout interview to increase interest in key stories

Four Parts of the Voice

Pace: speed up or slow down slightly, also use dramatic pauses to increase attention

Emotion/Timbre: (note – not a Pitbull song) this is the emotion you load in your voice, can be very effective at creating memorable stories

Chapter 8
Seated Posture, Eye Contact & Facial Expressions

I'm really critical of my posture, it makes a big difference. And I try to suck my belly in. Everyone should do that whether you're on a red carpet or not. Even if you're just going out to dinner with your boyfriend you should try and suck it in.
-Katy Perry

I have such a crush on Katy Perry, it's not even funny. If she says suck in your belly, I'll definitely do it. But seriously folks, posture is extremely important.

We've been discussing body language a lot so hopefully by now you're becoming aware of how important it is to be fully in control of the messages your non-verbal body language is sending.

A major part of that non-verbal message during an interview is going to be your posture. This includes how you hold yourself when you walk into the room, shake hands and sit down but most importantly, your posture during the interview.

Do you sit back, lean slightly to one side and cross your legs? Do you put your elbows on the table and rest your chin on your hands? How about clasping your hands behind your head and looking out the window?

Hopefully, you would never do any of the above in a professional interview. But how much thought do you put in to the way you're seated? It deserves some thought.

Start off strong

When you first walk in the room, stand tall and smile. Enter the room with confidence and that will be the first impression you make.

Give a good firm handshake, more on that in a later section, and introduce yourself in a slow, confident voice.

Now, let's be seated.

The first thing I do when I sit down is make sure the top of my back isn't resting against the top of the chair. If I am, I know I'm reclining too far back and the non-verbal body language I'm sending is too relaxed.

You should be excited to be there, ready to join the team. Sitting back makes you look like you've already got the job in the bag. And perhaps you do. But even if you do, you still don't want to convey that attitude.

Next thing is to position your feet flat on the floor pointing towards the interviewer. This forces the rest of your body to also be directly facing the interviewer which sends the non-verbal message that you're giving them you're full attention.

I don't recommend crossing the legs for guys, it's just too casual, too presumptive about the relationship.

However, women sometimes wear skirts and in that case it's perfectly acceptable to cross your legs professionally. However, still make sure your upper body is facing directly towards the interviewer to maintain the same attentive presence you would with your feet planted firmly on the floor.

Place your hands flat on your legs in a relaxed, comfortable manner. Don't rub your hands together or grab your fingers. This is a self-touch gesture meant to sooth your nerves and reveals nervousness or tension. Exactly the wrong kind of message to send. Keep your hands calm and relaxed unless you're making hand gestures and then return them to your legs calmly.

Use your face and eyes all the time

Now let's focus on your facial expressions and eye contact. Regarding facial expressions, smile. Smile more than you probably do on a normal basis. A smile shows confidence, it helps relax other people and it's an easy way to establish rapport with someone.

But when you're not smiling, you're an active listener. This means you nod occasionally to indicate you understand what the other person is saying. It means you keep your eye contact up and on the interviewer, not elsewhere. A good rule of thumb for eye contact is that you should keep good eye contact with the interviewer about 70% of the time.

Another good sign of active listening is to paraphrase back some of the questions you're asked to make sure you understood the question properly. This has the dual effect of not only letting the other person know that you're listening but also giving you a few seconds to think about your answer.

Don't be afraid to use your face to express emotions when you're telling your stories. Show surprise, fright, anger, joy and other emotions using your face. You don't need to be overly dramatic with this, just enough to make your point. This will make the stories much more entertaining and memorable.

And finally, always remember to sit up straight. Like Katy Perry said, suck in your belly. Keep your neck and

The Proper Seated Position

- Keep eye contact up and attentive
- Direct eye contact with the interviewer about 70% of the time

- Don't lean against the top of the chair, leave some space
- Sit up straight
- Head in line with your spine

- Hands flat on your thighs
- Don't rub or tap your fingers, keep your hands relaxed
- If hands are on a desk or table, tent your fingers together or loosely cross your fingers

- Feet flat on the floor with your toes pointing towards the interviewer
- Don't cross your legs, it's too casual
- Exception – ladies may cross their legs but maintain a seated position that directly faces the interviewer

Be an active listener!

Chapter 9
Hand Gestures

The hand is the visible part of the brain.
-Immanuel Kant

I've mentioned the importance of hand gestures previously but it's another area worth repeating. Effective hand gestures can be a great way to add emphasis and make your stories more memorable. The hands can really help us explain stories well and add visual depth to our message.

However, if the hands are used constantly and never come down, they become like annoying white noise on your television. Too much movement and your hands will become a subtle distraction for the interviewer and cause them to tune out.

I had a buddy who once told me, "In my culture and in my neighborhood especially, we like to talk with our hands. We use them all the time and we all know the gestures we're using. My mom used to say that if she wanted me to shut up she'd make me sit on my hands."

While I understand the cultural traditions that some have involving lots of hand gestures, I really think you'll be better served if you learn to edit them a bit. Once you do, you'll find out that less is more in this case.

Bring them up, use them, make them meaningful, then take them back down and calmly place them on your legs for a while. Give your hands and the interviewer a break once in a while.

Try to keep your hand gestures "in the box" as illustrated on the next page. If you need to make big gestures to make a point, do so. Just don't do it too often or it's like screaming at someone with your hands.

Hand Gestures in the Box

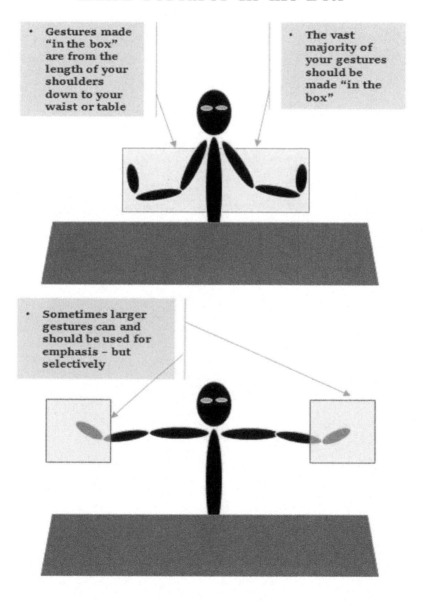

- Gestures made "in the box" are from the length of your shoulders down to your waist or table

- The vast majority of your gestures should be made "in the box"

- Sometimes larger gestures can and should be used for emphasis – but selectively

Part 3
Handshakes, Questions, Pressure and Practice

It's the little details that are vital. Little things make big things happen.
-John Wooden

In the final part of this book, I want to pull it all together by talking about some of the basic things we can do to increase our probability of interview success.

Sometimes we spend a lot of time and effort preparing for the major elements of an interview and we forget to consider some of the small details.

For example, how well do you shake hands? Do you have a weak, limp-wristed hand shake? Or are you a death-gripper who's squeezing everyone's hand too hard?

And when you leave the interview, what do you say? Do you just say thanks and walk out or could there be a way to make that moment more impactful and memorable.

Thus far we've been developing our knowledge about the company, the job, ourselves and how we're going to structure our background into great stories.

Then we discussed how we're going to use great verbal and non-verbal cues to emphasize certain parts of our stories and make them more memorable.

Now I want to spend some time talking about some of the basics that are often overlooked. Things like a good handshake, the questions you'll need to ask them towards the end of the interview, how to stay cool under pressure and how to practice.

Sometimes these can seem like trivial details that people don't really notice. You might think, "So what if you gave a weak handshake?"

Or perhaps, "The questions I ask them don't really matter, it's the way I answer their questions that count."

Unfortunately, this is not the case. Interviewers on Wall Street are watching for and observing everything. From the second you enter the room you are being evaluated. Things like your handshake, your smile, the manner in which you sat down – did you drop into your chair like a ton of bricks or did you sit down in a calm, controlled manner – all matter.

They want to see if you look the part, if you'll fit in to their tribe and be able to function successfully in their culture.

Yes, they are looking at your experience, your academic career, your market knowledge and other technical factors but they're probably more interested in you as a person.

Which means they're going to be paying attention and analyzing everything including handshakes, eye contact, the questions you ask and lots of other big and small details.

Remember, practice makes all of this easier, so after reading each section, practice and think about your own delivery.

Chapter 10
Handshakes

To build your self-image, you need to join the smile, firm handshake and compliment club.
                                    -Zig Ziglar

One small detail that is often overlooked but certainly should not be is a good, firm handshake.

From my experience running interviews, out of ten candidates, I would usually only get good handshakes from about five of them. The other five would be some variation of a weak hand with fingers extended like the Queen, a death grip wrapped around my fingers or a weak, cold, sweaty palm.

There are many other variations on the standard handshake but those three were the most common I have experienced during interviews.

A bad handshake is a terrible way to start and later end the interview. It probably (hopefully) won't cost you the job but why take the risk. Spend a few minutes practicing this common business interaction.

Here are two worst things to avoid with the basic handshake. First, don't give a weak, limp-wristed light grip. It's creepy and will leave a weird impression.

Second, don't overcompensate by giving the death grip around the other person's fingers. No one wants to have their hand squeezed too hard.

Instead, let's get back to the basics.

Handshake Basics

- **Three to five seconds**

- **The "U" between each person's thumb and index fingers are touching**

- **Thumbs wrapped around the top of the opposite hand**

- **Both participants squeeze using approximately the same pressure**

- **Both hands are perpendicular to the ground with neither party assuming the palm down dominant grip**

It's very simple but I know a lot of people out there aren't using these basics. If you are doing something other than the above, find a friend and practice on them. Ask them their opinion and see if you can make any adjustments which improve your effectiveness.

Index Finger Point Method

What if the problem isn't that you give people the death grip but that they typically give it to you? Some people tell me that for some reason they always seem to end up in handshakes where the other person is crushing their hand.

There is nothing worse than having someone grab your hand around your fingers and squeeze too early. This creates the finger death grip where one person has a solid grip on fingers and the other person is likely in pain.

I'm told this happens to women with petite hands quite often.

There is a solution to counter this bad handshaking trait, it's called the index finger point method. This is how it works:

Index Finger Point Method

- **As you go in for the handshake, point your index finger straight ahead with your index finger parallel to the ground**

- **As your hands get close, keep pointing your index finger straight down the person's wrist**

- **Once you start to grip, keep your index finger pointing and as high along the inside of the other person's arm as you can**

> **If you do this properly, it's practically impossible for them to get the death grip. Again, try this out on a friend a few times and get a feel for it.**

The "I'm the boss" handshake

Sometimes you'll go to shake someone's hand and they'll come at you with their palm down. Make no mistake, this is a sign of dominance. The person coming in with their palm down is asserting dominance.

The question to you is do you try to counter this and move the handshake to a more equal, both hands perpendicular to the ground? Or do you accept their dominance and shake hands with your palm slightly up.

The answer will depend on who the person is and the situation at the time. For the purposes of most interviews, it's probably a good idea to stroke the boss's ego and allow them the palm down handshake.

But again, you'll have to be the judge of this based on your individual situation.

Eye contact, smile and body spacing

It's important during your handshake that you maintain good eye contact, give your counterparty a nice smile and keep your body space a comfortable not-too-close/not-too-far distance.

You might be wondering how close is too close or how far too far?

To some extent this will vary according to your own cultural context. I'm American so I try to be neither too up-close and personal nor too cold and distant.

Some cultures have a reputation for allowing less personal space which means handshakes may have the participants standing very close to each other.

Other cultures are less personal and demand more space between participants to show respect.

Since this can vary a lot, try to understand your counterparty and what their expectations might be and then try to match that.

Small but important

Even though this is a very simple, quick part of the overall interview process, don't overlook it as meaningless. It is not. It is very important.

The handshake sends a non-verbal cue about who are you in the beginning of the interview. At the end of the interview, it helps reinforce the confident message you've been discussing throughout.

A bad handshake undermines all of that.

A good handshake solidifies it.

Chapter 11
What Questions Should You Ask Them?

Asking the right questions takes as much skill as giving the right answers.
                                            -Robert Half

I'll never forget one interview I had with an executive at Bear Stearns who asked me if I had any questions for him. I asked him if the rumors were true that Ace Greenberg used to give everyone a box of paper clips and tell them to make it last their entire time at Bear Stearns.

The man started smiling and for the next 30 minutes proceeded to tell me stories about Ace and how true this old story was. The executive really enjoyed recalling those days and the interview went over by about 15 minutes.

I'm not sure if it was my academic experience, work experience or the fun he had with this answer but the executive recommended me for the final round. I eventually received an offer from Bear Stearns but opted to work at Deutsche Bank instead.

In most investment banking interviews, the executive should be asking you most of the questions for the majority of the interview. However, there is usually time towards the end of the interview for you to ask the interviewer two or three questions. Have at least this many prepared when this opportunity arises.

Keep in mind, this is an important time in the interview. You have been given a chance to drive the bus. How will you do it? Safely, by keeping things on the road, highlighting your superior driving skills? Or will you go over a cliff?

Don't ask the obvious

Let's start by identifying the obvious that you don't want to ask them things that can be easily found by a quick trip to Google. Don't ask them who their current CEO is or what the stock price is or where the company sees itself in the future.

All of this should be on their website or researchable in some other way. As mentioned before, asking these questions also demonstrates that no matter what you've been saying about your interest in the company or industry, you clearly don't know what you're talking about. Asking basic questions is suicide.

Instead, a good tip is to focus on things that are more personal to the interviewer.

- *How did they get their job at the company?*
- *How did they decide on their current desk or role?*
- *What have the most successful summer interns done to make a good impression?*
- *What did some of the failures do that caused them to fail?*

Everyone loves to tell personal stories about themselves, especially after patiently listening to you for 30 minutes or more. Many people are ready to talk so give them the opportunity and tee up two or three nice questions that allow them to highlight their own skills and talents.

Chapter 12
The Closer's Question

Fortuna Fortes Juvat - Fortune Favors the Bold
-Motto of the 3rd Marine Regiment, United States Marine Corps

The next section we're going to discuss is one I consider to be one of the most important parts of the entire interview. This is when, in my opinion, you take a good interview and make it great.

Earlier in my career I was a credit derivative salesman at Deutsche Bank Securities in New York City. I covered all the big monoline insurance companies like MBIA, AMBAC, FGIC, FSA, XL, Assured Guaranty and CIFG. I bought CDS protection from them on CDOs, CMBS, RMBS and other structured products.

Quite an alphabet soup eh? Welcome to Wall Street.

In addition to my sales coverage, I also ran Deutsche Bank's recruiting efforts for the MBA program at NYU Stern.

A big part of that role was interviewing the dozens of applicants who applied to our summer intern and full-time associate programs to narrow the list down to the top 25-30 applicants.

Once I had done this, we would go interview those 25-30 students at NYU Stern's campus on Washington Square Park. The tough part with all this is that most of the students were very similar in terms of the academic backgrounds and work experience. The difference between many candidates was marginal.

This pool would be further narrowed down to the top ten who would be invited to our offices at 60 Wall Street for a Super Saturday interview session. They would meet three or four managing directors that day and they would decide the top four or five who would get offers.

So what gave someone the edge?

The people that got the offers were typically the people that stood out in a positive way from the crowd. They had more passion and demonstrated a dynamic presence. They asked better questions and seemed like they would be a good fit with our culture.

While I've talked in previously about some of the verbal and non-verbal cues you can use to stand out and be memorable, I want to discuss a question that I think all candidates should be asking at the end of every interview, the Closer's Question.

ABC – Always Be Closing

It has always been helpful for me to imagine the interview process as a sales process where the candidate is the product and the employer is the client. If you think about it, the two processes are very similar.

In the sales process you outreach to a large number of potential clients to try and generate interest in your product or service. Once you get some interest, you follow a series of carefully planned steps to meet the client, engage the client with what you're doing and try to gain the client's approval to purchase your goods.

This is essentially the same process you'd follow if you were doing an active job search.

However, I've noticed that there is one key element missing from most interviews that almost always happens during a sale – at some point in time you have to ask for the business, you have to close the deal.

In the sales process, it's almost always the salesperson that initiates the close. During the interview process, however, most interviewees fail to close the sale or even try.

But how would that work? How should the interviewee take the initiative and try to close (or at least soft close) the interview process?

Good questions at the end

Let's say most interviews last for 45 minutes. Towards the end of that time, it's typical for the interviewer to say something like, "Do you have any questions for me?"

As we discussed in the previous chapter, this is an opportunity for the interviewee to step up and drive the bus for a moment and should not be wasted.

Again, don't ask obvious questions that can be answered easily on Google like, "What are the different divisions of the firm?" or "What's your firm's mission statement?"

Instead, ask insightful questions about the role you're seeking, the culture of the firm or how the interviewer came to work at the firm and her experiences there. These questions are relatively safe, can provide you with good insight and lets the interviewer know you are thinking about the finer aspects of your employment like culture and fit.

I typically recommend candidates be prepared to ask at least two questions and maybe three.

Since the interview is almost over and the interviewer is answering questions, the dialog here tends to be a bit less formal and more personal. In other words, you've got them right where you want them.

Now you're at that moment when you've asked a few questions and she's dutifully answered them. The next thing to likely happen is the interviewer will stand up, thank you for your time, shake your hand and end the interview.

Fortune favors the bold

Instead, just before this happens, consider asking the closer's question for interviews:

"Thank you so much for meeting with me today. We've spoken for the last 45 minutes or so and you've had the chance to review my resume and speak with me about my background. Is there anything about my candidacy that you think will keep me from moving to the next round or getting the offer?"

My guess would be that some of you reading this are thinking, "No way, that's too aggressive."

Actually yes, in some ways it is aggressive. The process doesn't normally go like this. You are actively shaking things up and doing so in a way that could make some people uncomfortable.

But you're also doing something that will make you more memorable and you're definitely showing the interviewer that you really care about your candidacy. This helps underline the passion you may bring to their firm.

And quite frankly, most firms like to hire people that take the initiative and speak up. To me this is a bit like

Sheryl Sandberg's Lean In concept. Don't just sit back and let things happen, be an active participant in the outcome.

Personally, I don't see a lot of downside in the question. If the person actually does tell you that there was something wrong with your background then you now have one final opportunity to address it.

Interviewer: "I'm just not sure you have the quantitative skills to handle this role."

Candidate: "I hear your concern. Perhaps I didn't go deeply enough into my undergraduate background. I have actually completed three courses in Calculus and received an A in all three."

But to be fair, the interviewer almost never tells you there was something wrong. It's far more likely that they'll simply say, "No concerns, thank you so much for coming in today." And then end the interview.

Don't be afraid to stand out from the crowd

But perhaps you don't feel comfortable asking such a bold question. If that's the case, then definitely don't do it, you'll seem awkward rather than confident and it could fall flat.

Or perhaps you don't mind the question but would prefer to ask it in a different way. That's great, reword the question exactly as you think it should sound coming from your mouth.

Remember that a big part of the process here is standing out from the crowd. Who can sell themselves (the product) better than anyone else?

And if it's the right thing for salespeople to always be closing, why not for job applicants?

Chapter 13
Mock Interviewing and Using Video to Practice

The harder I practice, the luckier I get.
-Gary Player

Now we get to the fun part – practice, practice, practice. While it's best to practice with a friend, it's absolutely not necessary.

Conduct a mock interview for 10 mins, then 15, then 30. Finally work your way up to 45 minutes to one hour. It would be highly unusual to interview for longer than one hour but if you did, it probably means the firm is interested and is actually trying to sell you - a high class "problem" to have.

Become a director

First off, go on to amazon.com and buy a small tripod to mount your cell phone on to use during your video sessions. Anything simple will do. The tripods pictured below can all be purchased for under $10. As long as it allows you to get good video of your work, it should be fine.

To get started with your mock interview training, find a friend that's willing to help you or is also looking for a job and needs the practice as well.

Set up your video camera or phone and arrange the chairs so that the scenario resembles an office where you might interview. Another tip is to dress appropriately. At least wear business casual but if you should probably practice a few times in your suit or interview clothes. The more you can put yourself into the actual situation the better.

Get into character and stay in character

Once you've got the space all set up, leave the room for a minute, collect your thoughts and take a deep breath. Now knock on the door and have your partner welcome you in to the room just like the way things will work the day of your interview.

Enter the room and greet the person in exactly the same way as you will on interview day. Shake hands, exchange pleasantries and sit down. Again, just like you will at your actual interview.

The key here is behaving exactly as you will on the day of the interview. It's very important that you don't break character, stay in the role the entire time, especially when you mess up. Those are some of the most important learning lessons. Definitely take note of the times in your interview when you struggled and lost your place.

What you're trying to do here is two-fold. On the one hand you're going to be practicing the answers and the presentations style we've been working on in the previous section. How well do you know your stories?

How effectively are you making eye contact, smiling and using effective hand gestures?

On the other hand, you're also trying to practice getting used to the stress of the interview process.

It's one thing to come up with some great stories and then use body language and a strong voice that make those stories pop. It's quite another to do all of that in front of another person.

This is when you start to realize that interviewing is really just another form of public speaking.

Get an audience

Your audience is typically much smaller, one or two people interviewing you and you're sitting instead of standing. But almost everything else you need to be good at public speaking has to be present in the interview.

Now let's think about public speaking for a second. It's not easy, it's hard. For most people it's their number one fear in life. If you were asked to give a speech in public, you'd practice. Probably a lot.

And practicing alone in your bedroom in front of your mirror or with a video camera is great, but at some point you'll want to gather a small group of people and practice in front of them to get used to the feeling of presenting in front of people.

An interview should be no different, you have to practice in front of others to really get used to your delivery, timing, body language and everything else that goes into making the interview special.

Learn to fly solo

It's not likely that you'll always have a friend around who's a good mock interview partner. When this happens, get out your small tripod, pull up your phone's video camera and film yourself.

Ask the question you want to answer out loud and then give your answer. The reason for this is timing. Get used to listening to the answer first, gathering your thoughts for a second or two and then answering.

Even though you don't have another partner around to help you, you still want to practice the timing as if the person is there.

Review your video, it tells you no lies

Whether you're with a friend or practicing alone, once you've finished practicing on film, go watch the video. Stream it to your TV so you really get a sense of your body language and voice.

The first few times you do will be a little uncomfortable. I can already hear many of you saying, "I don't sound like that," or "That doesn't even look like me."

This discomfort with your appearance on video is natural and will fade with time. Don't worry, that is you and you do sound like that. Get over it and start to think critically and analytically about what you're doing.

How do your hand gestures look? Are you bringing them down sometimes or are they up the entire time?

How are your facial gestures and eye contact? Are you smiling? Are you making good eye contact with the interviewer about 70% of the time? Does your eye contact and facial expression look like someone who is actively listening?

How is your body language? Turn the volume down on your TV and watch your video with no sound. What kind of body language are you showing? Do you look nervous? Too casual? Hyper and tense?

How does your voice sound? Are you using a lot of filler words like "uh" and "um"? Are you talking too fast? Are you talking too slow? Are you varying your tone and adding emotion at the right time to enhance your stories?

And how do your stories sound? Are they too long? Do they accurately communicate the trait you're trying to express? Are they memorable? What can you do to edit each story into an even better version?

Chapter 14
Stay Cool Under Pressure: 6 Tips to Help You Stay Calm

> *Be like a duck, paddling and working very hard inside the water, but what everyone sees is a smiling and calm face.*
> *-Manoj Arora, From the Rat Race to Financial Freedom*

Don't let them see you sweat.

Imagine you're in a cab in Manhattan in the middle of August and it is hot and humid outside. The air conditioning in your cab is broken, your meeting is in Midtown in 10 minutes and you're Downtown stuck in traffic that isn't moving.

For most people, this means you're going to be sweating. If you're anything at all like me, you're going to be sweating a lot! My chest, back and under arms of my shirt are going to be soaked through and I'm going to have sweat pouring down my face.

Or what if you're just really nervous? Maybe this makes you sweat a lot also.

Or perhaps you don't sweat much but the nervousness still throws off your game.

Attractive image right? Employers are always looking to hire sweaty, nervous people aren't they?

Hardly, that's exactly the kind of hot mess you don't want to present as your first impression at an interview. You're going to be flustered and your confidence is going to be lower than it should. You'll be distracted during the interview wondering if the person is noticing and thinking about your sweating.

You get the idea. This is obviously a situation you want to avoid at all costs.

However, if you do find yourself in this situation, what's the best way to recover?

#1: **Be smart, plan ahead**

The easiest and first thing you can do is plan ahead. Think about how far the interview or meeting is from you and calculate how long you think it will take you in bad traffic. Now add 15-30 minutes to that and use it as your departure time.

These early departure times, however, will vary greatly depending on where you live. In New York City, an extra 15-30 minutes is usually fine. If you live in place with particularly bad traffic like Sao Paulo, Beijing or Mumbai, you might want to leave one to two hours early. Use your best judgement based on local conditions.

Best case scenario is you arrive at your destination a bit early. As mentioned earlier, if you're a coffee drinker, go grab a coffee somewhere to get the caffeine going. This will help perk you up just before you go in. If you don't like coffee, consider something else with caffeine or perhaps a chocolate bar for a quick energy burst.

But let's say despite your best efforts you still arrive in a rush with sweat rolling down your face.

What next?

#2: Pulse points – let the cooling begin

The best thing you can do if you're hot and sweaty is to calm down. Do this by finding a bathroom and putting some cold water on a few of your pulse points.

The first is the underside of your wrists. Turn the tap on cold and place your wrists under the cold water for 10-15 seconds. This will have a calming effect on your mind and will begin to allow your body to cool.

Another good pulse point is on the side of your neck below your ear. Put some cold water on your hands and rub a little on your neck. Be careful, however, and avoid getting your shirt or blouse wet.

If possible, and for guys this may be difficult with long-sleeved shirts, but you can also put some water on the inside of your elbows as this is another good pulse point that can help you cool down.

#3: Yoga breaths in and out of your nose

I mentioned this earlier in Chapter 2 and it's definitely important enough to be repeated. Yoga breaths are your best friend.

For years now I have taken and taught hot yoga classes where the temperature in the room is regularly above 110 degrees. In the beginning I hated the heat and couldn't stop thinking about how hot I was which typically only caused me to get stressed, further increasing the heat I felt.

Eventually, I learned how to breathe in a way that helped me stay cool and calmed me down.

All you have to do is take long, slow breaths in your nose and release them out of your nose. No mouth breathing, just the nose.

Try this now sitting at your desk. Inhale in your nose for five long, slow seconds, then exhale out your nose but take even longer on the exhale, six to eight seconds.

These breaths go in and out through your sinus cavity and are helping to cool the blood that's pumping to your brain. This will immediately help you calm down which in turn lowers stress.

Also, taking the long slow breaths requires you to focus on your breathing and calm your mind which does wonders to help you cool down and relax.

#4: Get to know Amy Cuddy's Ted Talk

In the previous section on making a good first impression, I discussed the pride pose. This was something developed by Harvard Professor Amy Cuddy. If you've never watched Professor Cuddy's amazing Ted Talk on body language called, Your Body Language Shapes Who You Are, I highly recommend you do:

https://www.ted.com/talks/amy_cuddy_your_body_language_shapes_who_you_are

I play this video in every class I teach. She makes a lot of wonderful points about how your body language affects the chemicals in your body but I want to focus on one piece of advice she gives – going in to the bathroom and assuming a pose that looks like you won the 100-yard dash in the Olympics.

Yes, you read that correctly. The pose is called pride and it's done by standing with your feet squarely underneath you, shoulder width apart. Next you'll want to clinch your fists, stick both arms up in the air and slightly elevate your chin. Now let a big smile wash over your face.

If you're doing this or can imagine it, you'll realize you look like someone who just won a competition of some sort. Google an image of Usain Bolt, there are a lot of pictures of him standing like this as he wins so often.

Standing in this pose for one to two minutes will help you lower your stress hormone (cortisol) and help you increase your confidence hormone (testosterone). This is exactly what you want as you get ready for your interview.

Even though it may feel a bit awkward, do it. Stand there and really let your body feel this pose. You'll be glad you did.

#5: Go workout, move and break a sweat

As I mentioned above, my workout is hot yoga. I know a lot of other people these days who really love CrossFit. Some people like to go for long runs. This is all great.

Whatever your workout is, get up early on the day of your interview and go workout. Even if working out in the morning isn't your thing, believe me, you will feel so much better physically if you get up early and get your blood pumping straight away.

When I was in the Marine Corps we used to wake up at 5am every morning. By 5:20am we were already on the road for our morning run.

Did I love waking up that early to go workout so hard? No - certainly not at first. But you get used to it and eventually you begin to love it. You feel amazing all day and when it's time for bed you crash out and get an amazing night's sleep.

Wake up early, hit the gym and get those endorphins flowing.

#6: The power of positive thinking

Another item previously discussed is positive thinking. This is good for building confidence, calming down and generally just feeling better.

If you happen to walk past the Marble Collegiate Church (built in the 1600s) on 29th and 5th Avenue in Manhattan, you'll see a statue in the courtyard of Dr. Norman Vincent Peale who was the author of the amazing book, *The Power of Positive Thinking* back in 1952. This was required reading in my family when I grew up.

In case you haven't read the book, let me summarize it quickly, keep your thoughts positive and push out the negative. You become what you think about most often so today you want to think of yourself as the best candidate for a Wall Street job on the planet.

Sounds easy right? It's not, it's hard. Many of us are in the bad habit of doubting ourselves or thinking the worst will always happen.

Even if this is your mindset, try your best to consciously avoid it on your interview day. Think positive.

It's time

You have the skills, experience and work ethic needed to do great on the job. You know your resume and have great stories to bring it to life. You understand how you're using your body language and verbal cues to add impact. You know about the company you're meeting and have prepared extensively for this interview.

You'll want to have done research before your interview like a lawyer does before a trial. Not only do you know most of the questions and answers in advance, you know the best way to present them to the jury.

Take the time to really understand your stories and how to tell them for the maximum impact.

Organize your schedule so you can do your research, write your stories, practice your delivery, network with industry contacts, arrange informational interviews and still live a happy life, whatever that means to you.

By the way, that's what financial professionals do. Many of them work extremely long hours for years, decades in some cases. Even a light work load will be 65-70 hours and that will be the minimum hours worked in the early years.

If you're organized, disciplined, interested in finance and economics and intellectually curious, you could get your chance to work on the big deals and make the big bonuses. Your dream job on Wall Street is closer than you might think.

But you have to get there first. To get there you need more than goals, you need a system.

Don't tell me about your goals, tell me about the daily system you're using to work towards them.

That tells me all I need to know about your ability to accomplish goals. Using the 3x3 Interview Prep Method, you have all the tools needed to build a solid daily routine to prepare for your next big interview and accomplish your goal of working on Wall Street.

You're ready now.

Tell yourself that and believe it.

Now in a calm, cool, organized manner...

Go. Get. That. Job.

Afterword

The secret of getting ahead is getting started.
-Mark Twain

It has been a joy for me to write this book and scratch yet another item off my own personal bucket list.

I genuinely hope that my 3x3 Interview Prep Method of breaking down the interview process into easy, bite-sized chunks makes sense and is useful for you.

I have used this method for years and it has always successful. That doesn't mean I always get the job offer. That's a decision that can be influenced by things outside of my control, but I always put my best foot forward.

I have also taught this method to others who have gone out and realized great success with it in their own lives.

Finally, I started teaching these skills to the Masters of Science in Quantitative Finance students at Fordham University's Gabelli School of Business. After going through the basics of this program with the class, I realized a book on the subject could be helpful for a lot of people.

I would love to have your feedback. Please reach out to me on LinkedIn or get in touch with me via my website at www.rogersgroupnyc.net.

Thanks for reading and good luck with your next interview!

-Brian, 1/25/17

Index

Adams, Douglas. Hitchhikers Guide to the Galaxy. Del Rey, 2002.

Allen, David. Getting Things Done. Penguin Group, 2001.

Epictetus. The Art of Living. HarperCollins Publishers, 1994.

McLaughlin, Peter. Becoming the Customer. Dog Ear Publishing, 2013.

Peale, Dr. Norman Vincent. The Power of Positive Thinking. Touchstone, 2003.

Stephen Young, Stephen. MicroMessaging. McGraw Hill, 2007.

http://careers.workopolis.com/advice/study-how-quickly-do-interviewers-really-make-decisions (February 1, 2017)

https://www.ted.com/talks/amy_cuddy_your_body_language_shapes_who_you_are (February 15, 2017)

About the Author

Professor Brian Rogers has over 25 years of professional experience and is the founder and principal of theROGERSgroup nyc, a boutique consulting firm focused on improving the communication skills of executives at all levels.

In addition to his consulting work, Brian is also an adjunct professor of business communication at NYU's Stern School of Business and Fordham's Gabelli School of Business.

Brian currently lives in the Rose Hill neighborhood of Manhattan with his two children.

Made in the USA
Las Vegas, NV
14 January 2022